The No-Prep Bible Study Series

The Most Glorious Psalms Ever

What People Are Saying

"Kenny Beck has written a wonderfully simple book to help small groups study "The Most Glorious Psalms Ever." I love the way Kenny gives every small group leader questions that will promote discussion and bring insight to these beautiful Psalms."

> — Dr. Pat Sparks, Lead Pastor, St. Peter's United Methodist Church, Katy, Texas

"Kenny Beck is clearly utilizing his God-given gift as teacher as he takes us on a journey with thought-provoking lessons on some of the best-known Psalms. He facilitates understanding through simplified study, pointed discussion, and actionable takeaways that resonate with both mind and soul. Well done, Kenny, class dismissed!"

> —Chris Roberts, Vice President Mission Advancement, Living Water International

"Kenny's experience as both a Sunday School teacher and a music teacher complement each other in these lessons on Israel's songbook. His musical background allows him to draw attention to a different set of details and thoughts which will benefit others in appreciating and applying these Psalms."

> — Randy Hillebrand, Spreader of the Gospel, Eurasia and Asia

"Kenny Beck opens up some of the "Most Glorious Psalms Ever" for us. His easy-to-use Q&A format works well in getting us to applications that can change our lives and our communities."

> — Dr. Bobby V. Page, Missions and Care Pastor, River Pointe Church, Richmond, Texas (Chaplain, Brigadier General, USAF, Retired)

The No-Prep Bible Study Series

The Most
Glorious
Psalms Ever

Kenny Beck

Dedication

To my father, who allowed me to attend his adult Bible study as a teenager

Contents

Acknowledgements

Special thanks have to go first to my wife, Melissa, and daughter, Mallory. These two highly talented ladies have handled all the editing, layout, and artwork for this book. What you hold in your hands exists because of their ideas and handiwork.

Additionally, I'd like to give a quick nod to one Bible teacher in particular: Mark Lanier. I've absorbed a certain biblical perspective and viewpoint from listening online to Mark's world-renowned teaching in his long-running Biblical Literacy class at Champion Forest Baptist Church of Houston.

Finally, I must mention three pastors who have had a major impact on my spiritual life: the late Dr. John R. Bisagno, Ryan Rush, and Roy Meadows. All three of these men have inspired my spirit, enlightened my mind, and been a shining personal example to me.

The No-Prep Bible Study Series

The *No-Prep Bible Study Series* is designed to meet the needs of the untold thousands of small groups engaged in Bible study. They are known in the church world as Community Groups, Life Groups, Small Groups, Adult Bible Fellowships, and even by the old-fashioned name of, yes, Sunday School Classes.

By "no prep," we mean no preparation on the part of the **leader or the participants**. You can simply read the short text, answer the questions, and bring a **meaningful and focused** Bible study to conclusion in 45 minutes.

These studies are geared for Christians across denominational lines. Indeed, every study has been trial tested on real small groups from different denominations. Participants have invariably found these unique studies to be engaging and thought provoking.

Group Tips

- Your group should designate a leader to be in charge of three things:
  - Starting on time
  - Keeping it moving
  - Finishing on time

- Always check the given answers to make sure you stay on track.
- Be kind and don't let one person dominate.
- Budget 45 minutes and stick to it!

Also Available

- *Jesus' Most Popular Parables*

Planned for Release December 2020

- *Happiness v. Purpose*

Check for availability at either:

- NoPrepBibleStudies.com
- Amazon.com

A Quick Word
About the Psalms

Israel's Songbook

The 150 Psalms served as the songbook for the Jewish people in Old Testament times. Most of the Psalms contain important theological ideas—ideas about who God is, what He provides for us, and the praise we owe Him. But ultimately, each and every Psalm was first and foremost a song.

The Lyricists

We tend to think about our Bible in terms of its authors. But the writers of the Psalms would be better described as poets or songwriters or even lyricists. David quickly comes to mind as the principal psalmist. Indeed, 73 Psalms are attributed to David. But the other Hebrew poets who contributed to this ancient hymnal included Asaph, the sons of Korah, Solomon, Moses, and even some guy named Ethan.

The Styles and Tunes

Many of the Psalms have interpretive musical inscriptions at the beginning. While these inscriptions are often linguistically uncertain, many scholars think that the wild Hebrew words are describing the style of the music. A few inscriptions even name a tune. For instance, Psalm 22 is set to the tune of "The Doe of the Morning." And Psalm 60 is to be sung to the tune of "The Lily of the Covenant."

The Instruments

We get a decent picture of the instruments of the ancient Hebrews from Psalm 150. The Israelites had some little flutes and some rams' horns. But mainly there were stringed instruments—think harps and lyres. And as for the percussion section, tambourines and cymbals were used. (The drummer guy in the plexiglass cage had not yet been invented.)

As we look mainly at the important theology undergirding our chosen Psalms, hopefully you can keep in the back of your mind that these were actual songs sung in ancient Israel. Now, turn in your hymnal to Psalm 100!

1

Psalm 100
Thanksgiving

Psalm 100

A Psalm for giving thanks.

[1]Make a joyful noise to the Lord, all the earth!

    [2]Serve the Lord with gladness!

    Come into his presence with singing!

[3]Know that the Lord, he is God!

    It is he who made us, and we are his;

    we are his people, and the sheep of his pasture.

[4]Enter his gates with thanksgiving,

    and his courts with praise!

    Give thanks to him; bless his name!

[5]For the Lord is good;

    his steadfast love endures forever,

    and his faithfulness to all generations.

The Study

Thanksgiving Traditions

For me, Thanksgiving Day has always been about the three Fs: family, food, and football. We are a fairly typical American family. All of us, young and old, gather at my sister's house to eat Thanksgiving dinner, cavort together, and root for the Dallas Cowboys. (Forgive us, we're from Texas!)

Our dinner is also fairly typical—turkey and dressing and lots of side dishes. My sister's specialty side is our favorite—skinny green beans, wrapped in bacon, drenched in butter, and held together with a toothpick. It is good to have sisters! And of course, there are the requisite pies. Pecan pies, pumpkin pies, apple pies.

After dinner, family members continue to socialize. Some play games: dominoes, foosball, Madden. Some doze on the couch. Some walk around the neighborhood—trying to walk off all those slices of pie.

But when the Cowboys game starts, everyone reconvenes around the big TV to root for our favorite football team. The Dallas quarterbacks have changed over the years…Morton, Staubach, Aikman, Romo, Prescott. Our devotion has not.

1. What Thanksgiving traditions does your family have?

I intentionally saved the centerpiece of our family's Thanksgiving traditions for last. You see, before each Thanksgiving dinner, we gather round in a circle and read Psalm 100. This tradition has been going on since I can remember. Let's call it 50+ years.

Nowadays, my mother is the ranking matriarch and does the honors, usually adding a few minutes of her fabulous teaching and exhortation.

Please open your heart and mind today to this very short and simple Psalm. As we consider its main thrust of thanksgiving and gratitude, it will likely change your mindset, and maybe even your daily actions. Plus, you might even consider adding a Psalm 100 reading to your Thanksgiving traditions.

Theology First

The underlying structure to Psalm 100 is:

- Our actions—vv. 1-2
- Theology—v. 3
- Our actions—v. 4
- Theology—v. 5

Go ahead and put boxes around verses 3 and 5 and label them "theology." That will help you see the structure.

Read Psalm 100:1-5

2. What is the theological statement at the beginning of v. 3?

3. What is the theological statement at the beginning of v. 5?

The first and main theological statements are clearly **"He is God,"** creator of humankind, and **"He is Good."** There's plenty more fantastic theology in those verses, and no doubt you saw that sheep/shepherd analogy fly by. We will save the Good Shepherd analogy for the upcoming Psalm 23 lesson. But for now, let's proceed on to what Psalm 100 instructs us to specifically do.

Action Second

Re-read Psalm 100:4.

4. What is our main action of v. 4?

Verse 4 is the verse that leads almost every translation to label Psalm 100 as "A Psalm of Thanksgiving."

5. Do vv. 1-2 also have a call to thanksgiving and praise?

Notice that we have thanksgiving explicit in v. 4 and at least implied in vv. 1-2.

6. What is the little connective word at the beginning of v. 5?

Hence, our thanksgiving action is tied to God's goodness and his steadfast love.

7. Is the pronouncement to "give thanks" in v. 4 more of a command, encouragement, invitation, or response?

So, we apparently have a command to give thanks to the Lord because "He is God," and because "He is Good."

But does the average Christian overflow with thanksgiving and thankfulness? I'm not so sure. Have we perhaps relegated thankfulness to a one-day-a-year ritual? And mixed it with a good dose of football? Let's look closer at thankfulness, or gratitude, if you will. Let's make sure we aren't somehow accidentally neglecting this Christian virtue.

Ingratitude—The Cause

It is likely that many Christians don't overflow with thankfulness and gratitude to the Lord. I know that I didn't till a few years ago when I was convicted about it and took action.

8. Do you think man's natural state is one of gratitude or ingratitude? Which way do we tend to go?

It's probably safe to say that most of us aren't as grateful as we should be. The first thing we need to do is see if we can figure out what causes ingratitude.

9.   How do you think ingratitude creeps into our lives?

I personally believe that ingratitude seeps into our lives in a sneaky two-step process. See if you can fill in the blanks.

- First, we get used to what we _____
- Then, we take it for _____

To me, that kind of gives us the bare bone essentials of ingratitude. We get used to what we **have** and then we begin taking it for **granted**. That's what leads us to a lack of thanksgiving to the Lord. With that critical understanding, let's look for solutions.

Ingratitude—The Solution

A few years ago, I ran into four small books in fairly rapid succession that all preached the exact same message on how to intentionally build thankfulness into your life. Those four little positive books are:

- *Thank You Power*[1]
- *Don't Sweat the Small Stuff*[2] (Get this book!)
- *Powered by Happy*[3]
- *Positive Dog*[4]

Very succinctly, here's the get-it-done advice on thankfulness espoused by all four books:

- **Focus on what you have, not on what you want**
- **Give thanks to God for the little things you have**

Now there's some quick actionable items!!! The first one alters your mindset. The second one primes the pump and gets you started. And both fight our human tendency of getting used to the things we have and taking them for granted.

Before we get you started making lists of really itty-bitty little things to thank the Lord for, allow me to share a pretty dramatic example in my own life.

I'm a Sunday School teacher by calling, but a piano teacher by trade. Indeed, I've taught 40-60 piano students every week for the past 35 years. A few days before Christmas in 2011, I injured my left index finger. Over the next several weeks, that injury gradually left me with a little ball of scar tissue right at the end of the bone in the tip of the finger. To strike a piano key with that left index finger now brought a jolt of pain. I could use the finger most every other way, but just not to play the piano. Basically, I was now a 9-fingered piano teacher. Not good!

The Lord eventually led me to a piano-playing hand surgeon. This talented lady thought she could go in on the side of the finger and remove that ball of scar tissue without tearing up the finger too bad. She skillfully operated and restored my left index finger. Praise the Lord!!!

I tend to pray while walking. And as you might imagine, nowadays, I begin every prayer-walk thanking the Lord for each and every finger, touching each one as I go. I stop on that left index finger and thank the Lord for that surgeon by name. That is just the beginning of my thanking the Lord for tons and tons of little things in my life, things that I had so easily taken for granted before.

Priming the Pump

Let's get the ball rolling right now. Think of some really little things that you've gotten used to and have taken for granted. **The littler the better.** Things like your fingers, your knees, your eyes. Things like your shoes, your shampoo, your toothbrush. Things like your cereal, your Starbucks, your peanut butter. People like your auto-mechanic, your chiropractor, your A/C guy. The list is endless.

10. List 10 **little things** you can thank God for.

11. List 5 **big things** you can thank God for.

12.   List 3 **big spiritual blessings** you can thank God for.

Hopefully, you see the way forward in having a heart full of thanksgiving. You don't start at the top with "Thank you, Lord, for saving my soul" and kind of peter out after that. You start at the bottom with lots of little things and crescendo up till you finally finish with "Thank you, Lord, for saving my soul!"

I hope this quick study of Psalm 100 will prod you into a lifestyle of more thanksgiving to the Lord. May you and I indeed enter His gates with thanksgiving, for the Lord is good and His steadfast love endures forever.

My Answers

Question 1

Your traditions

Question 2

He is God

Question 3

He is Good

Question 4

Thanksgiving, praise

Question 5

"Come into his presence with singing" tends to imply praise and thanksgiving. Indeed, one spritely little praise chorus from the 80s went like this: "Come into his presence with thanksgiving in your heart, and give him praise, and give him praise."

Question 6

"For" is that little connector word; it is very similar to "because."

Question 7

I kind of view it as a "command." But "response" has a lot of merit too.

Question 8

Man's natural state is ingratitude. That's the way we tend to go—some of us more than others.

Question 9

Various answers

Question 10

Your lunch sandwich, your shirts, your phone, your eye-glasses, your vitamins, your fingers, your teeth, your cat, your lawn-mower, your water filter, hot showers

Question 11

Your car, your house, your job, your kids, your wonderful neighborhood

Question 12

Salvation, the Holy Spirit, His steadfast love

2

Psalm 23
Relationship

Psalm 23

A Psalm of David.

[1]The Lord is my shepherd; I shall not want.
  [2]He makes me lie down in green pastures.
He leads me beside still waters.
  [3]He restores my soul.
He leads me in paths of righteousness
    for his name's sake.
[4]Even though I walk through the valley of the shadow of death,
    I will fear no evil,
for you are with me;
    your rod and your staff,
    they comfort me.
[5]You prepare a table before me
    in the presence of my enemies;
you anoint my head with oil;
    my cup overflows.
[6]Surely goodness and mercy shall follow me
    all the days of my life,
and I shall dwell in the house of the Lord
    forever.

The Study

Songwriting—Then & Now

Modern song writers build their songs around one main thing—**a hooky line.** You know—that catchy phrase that comes around again and again that forms the memorable core of the song.

In fact, the modern songwriting formula tends to be: find a hooky line, build a chorus around it, then create two or three verses that feed into the chorus.

Can I state the obvious?

The 150 Psalms in the Bible (yes, the Psalms were songs**!**) **were not built around hooky lines.** They are essentially Hebrew poetry—pairs of rhythmical poetic lines—infused with theology and praise. No repetitive choruses. No hooky lines.

But what did the Psalms actually **sound like**? And what were the melodies?

We don't know. Those melodies have long since been lost to history.

There is however one modern song that probably gives you some feel for what a Psalm may have sounded like 3000 years ago. It is "The Lord Is My Shepherd" by Keith Green. Keith's haunting and lilting 6/8 melody in C minor has a certain Hebrew feel. Plus, it matches Psalm 23 word for word! To his credit, Keith even chose the lofty tone and bouncy feel of the King James Version, with such phrases as "He restoreth my soul" and "Thou preparest a table before me."

There are plenty of other modern Psalm 23 songs. But they all have those invented hooky lines.

I encourage you to listen to Keith Green's "The Lord Is My Shepherd." It will likely give you some semblance of how Psalm 23 might have sounded in King David's court in 1000 BC. Of course, you have to use your imagination and strip away the piano and strings, leaving King David with his minimal harp accompaniment.

In any case, Psalm 23 is one of the most beloved and cherished Psalms in all of Christendom. Many would say it is **the most glorious Psalm ever**. I would not argue with them.

Do It How???

The plan for today's study is to approach Psalm 23, drum roll please...backwards! So far in my lengthy Bible teaching career, I've taught just four bible passages backwards—Psalm 23, 1 Corinthians 13, Isaiah 55, and Revelation. Yes, I've taught the book of Revelation backwards in 8 broad lessons. The series title was, get this, "Revelation Backwards!"

You might be dubious about this approach. But let me ask you a couple of probative questions.

1. Do you think you would see things differently if you walked around your block the opposite way than you normally do? Why?

2. What possible benefits are there to approaching a Bible passage backwards?

Let's get organized so we can tackle Psalm 23 **backwards**. Go ahead and put brackets on verses 1-4, then on verse 5, and then on verse 6, labeling them "Shepherd Metaphor," "Host Metaphor," and "Theological Core."

Let's jump in and do Psalm 23 backwards. See what you think.

Theological Core

Read Psalm 23:6.

Typically, this last verse gets little attention. By verse 6, we're usually kind of mentally tired and simply want to wrap up.

But David says a couple of super important things theologically here at the end of Psalm 23—one dealing with his current life and one dealing with his afterlife.

3. What two things does David say will be with him in this life?

4. Where does David say he will spend eternity?

Wow! God's goodness and mercy are in this life and eternal life afterwards! It doesn't get much bigger than that theologically. We could spend a lot of time here, but's let's press on, going backwards to verse 5.

The Host Metaphor

Read Psalm 23:5.

David's analogy—or metaphor—is foreign to modern Americans. "Preparing a table" describes the ancient Middle East custom of a rich person hosting a banquet for his lesser guests. Anointing a guest's head with oil was part of the welcoming process. And of course, after the lavish banquet, entertainment was sure to follow.

Just to make sure we make the proper metaphorical connections:

5. Who is the rich host?

6. Who is the lesser guest?

Yes, God is the rich host throwing that banquet for you, the lesser guest. The implication for you is threefold. First, God is your provider. Second, God puts you in a place of privilege. And third, you are the one who is blessed beyond all measure till your cup overflows.

Of course, all that is dependent upon your accepting the Lord's invitation and showing up for the banquet. Jesus seemed to be making exactly that connection in "The Parable of the Great Banquet" in Luke 14:15-24. You might remember that parable. Many of the invitees to that banquet made lame excuses and chose not to come.

But let's move backwards and finish with one of the most beloved passages in the entire Bible: "The Lord is my shepherd; I shall not want."

The Shepherd Metaphor

Read Psalm 23:1-4.

The whole first part of Psalm 23 is an extended metaphor where the Lord is the shepherd and David is the little sheep that gets taken care of. Hence, there are shepherding words and terms sprinkled throughout these four verses. Let's find all those shepherding terms and figure out what they represent.

7.   Where does the little sheep get to go in vv. 1-2?

8.   What does that represent?

You might notice that in v. 3a, "restores my soul" is the only line that has no shepherding imagery.

9.   What does the shepherd actually do in v. 3b?

10. What does that represent?

11. What two shepherding tools are used on the little sheep at the end of v. 4?

12. The rod and staff are actually said to do what for the sheep?

So, I hope you've gone through all these shepherding verses making the connection that God **provides** for you, **guides** you, and **comforts** you—if indeed you are part of his flock.

Jesus Takes Over

In an extended discourse in John 10, Jesus took over this wonderful metaphor calling Himself the Good Shepherd and calling us His sheep. But the Lord took this metaphor way further than David did in Psalm 23. Jesus clearly frames his Shepherd/sheep analogy in John 10 as a **two-way relationship**:

Jesus speaks—We hear His voice

Jesus leads—We follow Him

Jesus knows us—We know Him

Let me throw out one final sobering thought. Not everyone is His sheep automatically. Christ said that rather bluntly in John 10:26. Only people who hear Him, follow Him, and know Him are His sheep.

Let's wrap up with an endearing little summer camp song drawn from Psalm 23: "In God's Green Pastures Feeding." Go ahead and circle on line 5 what Christ does for His sheep. And of course, make sure you have that two-way relationship with the Good Shepherd.

In God's green pastures feeding, by His cool waters lie,
Soft in the evening walk my Lord and I,
All the sheep of his pasture fare so wondrously fine,
His sheep am I.

O do you know the Savior who has died for the sheep?
Know of his cleansing blood, his power to keep?
He's a wonderful Savior and he loves you and me.
Are you his sheep?

My Answers

Question 1

Things will appear totally different. Just try it. Your eye will be drawn towards different things from different angles. Whenever I walk around my block backwards, I'm amazed at how different everything looks and feels.

Question 2

Approaching a Bible passage backwards can bring:

- Freshness to a familiar passage
- Likely, a new emphasis
- A new exit point leading to different concluding thoughts

Question 3

God's goodness and God's mercy. The underlying Hebrew words are "tob" and "hesed." Interestingly, "tob" and "hesed" are the underlying Hebrew words to the theological ending of Psalm 100 also. Those words are just translated a little differently as "good" and "lovingkindness." But it is worthy to note that David finishes both Psalm 23 and 100 talking about God's goodness and mercy.

Question 4

In the house of the Lord forever = with God throughout eternity. However, it should be noted that not all Bible scholars are in agreement on this interpretation. Some feel like David is still talking about his life here on earth.

Question 5

God is the rich host

Question 6

You are the lesser guest—provided that you show up for the banquet

Question 7

- Green pastures = nice grazing places
- Still waters = nice drinking places

Question 8

It represents God's provision for his people

Question 9

- The shepherd leads the sheep down good paths. Also note: the path can also be a dark and dangerous path as alluded to in v. 4—"the valley of the shadow of death." The Hebrew there is very hard to put into words, but the meaning is along the lines of a bad, dark path.

Question 10

It represents God's guidance for his people.

Question 11

- The rod – to beat off predator animals
- The staff—to hook around the neck of the little wandering sheep and bring him back to safety

Question 12

David defines this analogy. He says the rod and staff comfort the sheep.

3

Psalm 19
Progressive Revelation

Psalm 19

A Psalm of David.

[1]The heavens declare the glory of God,
    and the sky above proclaims his handiwork.
[2] Day to day pours out speech,
    and night to night reveals knowledge.
[3] There is no speech, nor are there words,
    whose voice is not heard.

[7] The law of the Lord is perfect,
    reviving the soul;
the testimony of the Lord is sure,
    making wise the simple;
[8] the precepts of the Lord are right,
    rejoicing the heart;
the commandment of the Lord is pure,
    enlightening the eyes;

[14] Let the words of my mouth and the meditation of my heart
    be acceptable in your sight,
    O Lord, my rock and my redeemer.

The Study

Mother Knows Best

When I was a child, my mother made me and my two sisters make up our beds. And we couldn't be sloppy. It had to be hotel-like quality. Sheets tucked. Wrinkles smoothed out. Pillows fluffed up. Everything had to be just right.

1. What basic things did your mom make you do when you were a kid?

Of course, moms (and kids) come in all different temperaments. But, on average, most kids have to be made to do some pretty basic things. You know, things like brush your teeth, comb your hair, change your shirt, go to school! Without moms, this world would crash and burn.

But far and away, the most important thing my mom ever made me do was memorize Scripture. And one of the very first Scriptures I ever memorized was Psalm 19:1.

This majestic verse is more important than you probably realize. In fact, Psalm 19:1, along with Psalm 19:7 form two bedrock theological planks on a crucial topic—how God reveals himself to man.

Over the years, I ended up memorizing almost every verse in Psalm 19. My personal favorite is Psalm 19:14: "Let the words of my mouth, and the meditation of my heart, be acceptable in your sight, O Lord, my rock, and my redeemer." Even that verse is more important theologically than you might think.

Psalm 19 is definitely beautiful to our ears and our hearts, but it is also a theological powerhouse. To many Christians, me included, it is easily one of the most glorious Psalms ever.

Progressive Revelation

Most Christian theologians have noted that **God reveals himself to man more and more over time.** They've labeled this theological concept "progressive revelation." That term makes good sense. Let's analyze it.

The root of the word "revelation" is obviously "reveal." And just who is doing the revealing? God is, of course. God is revealing himself to man. That's really important! Because, in most other religions, man is trying to figure out God. This is quite simply a strong distinctive of Christianity. We believe that we don't figure out God, but that **God reveals himself to us.**

When we look at history and the Scriptures, we also notice that God did not reveal himself to us totally all at once. That might have blown us away! He chose to do it **incrementally over time.** That's what the word "progressive" means.

Basically, God has revealed himself to mankind in four steps, or levels, if you will. And that is our quest today: to see those four incremental levels in which God has revealed himself to us. Your main goal is to fill in the following progressive revelation chart as this study progresses:

Progressive Revelation

Level 1 = _____

Level 2 = _____ _____

Level 3 = _____ _____

Level 4 = _____ ____ _____

This is going to be simpler than you think and very understandable. Indeed, you have probably been subconsciously processing the Scriptures already through the prism of progressive revelation and just haven't realized it.

Let's jump in and tackle this glorious Psalm of David!

Creation Speaks

Read Psalm 19:1-3.

2. In verse 1, what is David referring to when he says "the heavens?"

So, the anchor noun of these three verses is "the heavens," meaning the sun, moon, stars, and planets.

I would argue that the anchor verb of these three verses is "speak." The New Living Translation (NLT)[5] goes with the word "speak" in vv. 2-3: "Day after day they continue to **speak**" and "They **speak** without a sound or word."

Actually, I find six words all centered on the concept of speech or speaking in verses 1-3. There is one on every line!

3.   Circle those six words dealing with speech or speaking in vv. 1-3.

So, "the heavens" are "speaking" to us.

4.   What exactly are the heavens telling us?

Yes, when we gaze into the heavens, we see God's glory and power on display.

Most study Bibles will give you a cross reference from Psalm 19:1 over to Romans 1:20. This is a crucial cross-reference. In Romans 1:20, Paul takes it a step further saying that **all of creation speaks to us.** Here it is in the NLT: "For ever since the world was created, people have seen the earth and sky. Through everything God made, they can clearly see his invisible qualities—his eternal power and divine nature." You get what Paul is saying. When you look at creation, it tells you that **God exists** and that **He is powerful.**

Two quick questions before we move on.

5.   What two optical inventions around 1600 allow us to "see" creation a whole lot better?

6.   Does one of those help us grasp God's power, glory, and existence more than the other? If so, which one—the telescope, or the microscope?

So creation itself is the basis of God's progressive revelation to mankind. Put "Creation" in as Level 1 in your chart, and let's move on to Level 2.

The Law Enlightens

In verse 7, David shifts gears away from creation over to a new topic— "the law of the Lord."

Read Psalm 19:7-8.

David uses four phrases to refer to the law: the law of the Lord, the testimony of the Lord, the precepts of the Lord, and the commandment of the Lord.

7.   What exactly is David referring to when he says "the law of the Lord?"

8.   Where exactly is the Mosaic law found in the Bible?

9.   What best known part of the Mosaic law was written in stone?

So, the "law of the Lord" is the Mosaic law found in Exodus through Deuteronomy, the core of which is the Ten Commandments.

10. What four things does David say the **law is**?

11. What four things does David say the **law does**?

Wow! Sounds like the Mosaic law was pretty special and a great guide for life. I think you caught the very last one. **The law enlightens us!** This implies that we learn some things when we encounter the Mosaic law.

Most Bible scholars say that the Mosaic law is indeed the next step up the ladder in God revealing himself to mankind. God reveals his holiness, his standards, and his proper place of preeminence in our lives. Along the way in that Mosaic covenant, He also reveals to us that we won't measure up to his standards and that a blood sacrifice is required to atone for our sins.

So, put "Mosaic law" in your chart as Level 2 of God's progressive revelation. And you already sense where we are going next. The next step is obviously Jesus Christ.

Jesus Shows

It almost goes without saying that God's best revelation of himself is Jesus Christ. But let's be good Bible students and throw out a supporting Scripture or two. Let's go to the very last verse of John's prologue to his gospel, John 1:18. In one paraphrase, John 1:18 reads: "No one has ever seen God. The only Son, who is the same as God and is at the Father's side, He has made Him known.[6]" Even with those confusing pronouns at the end, you probably see it. Jesus makes God the Father known to us! **Jesus reveals the Father.**

But just where does John come up with this theological thought of Jesus making the Father known to us? Where does John get it? He gets it from Jesus himself! Jesus said: "He who has seen me has seen the Father" (John 14:9).

In fact, 90% of the time, any theology expressed by the New Testament writers (Peter, Paul, James, John) can be traced directly back to the words of Jesus.

So go ahead and put "Jesus Christ" next on your chart of progressive revelation. Christ indeed shows us the nature and holiness and love of God much more than creation and the Mosaic law ever could.

Most theologians stop with Jesus Christ at Level 3. But I find there is one final level of God revealing himself to us.

Final Revelation

Ultimately, God will reveal himself fully to us in heaven when we see Him face to face. In Revelation 22:3-4, we find that "God's servants will see

His face." And then there is the much-loved verse from the apostle Paul, "For now we see in a mirror dimly, but then face to face" (1 Cor 13:12).

So, fill in that last and most wonderful level of progressive revelation— **face to face!**

A Cool Analogy

One way of conceptualizing the four levels of progressive revelation involves an analogy of four brighter and brighter sources of light. You can probably come up with this analogy yourself. Give it a go!

12. What are four brighter and brighter sources of light that we could use to relate to the four levels of progressive revelation? (Clue: The first one could be a candle.)

You might as well put your four light source analogies next to "Creation," "Mosaic law," "Jesus Christ," and "Face to Face" in your chart. Analogies are cool. But remember, they only exist to help us understand the real thing.

Wrapping Up

Let's finish back in Psalm 19.

Read Psalm 19:14.

13. What is the **very last word** in this Psalm?

14. How often do you see that word in the Old Testament?

That's right. The word "redeemer" is almost never seen in the Old Testament. We find redeem, redeemer, and redemption almost exclusively in the New Testament. Yet David uses it here. And he personalizes it— **my** redeemer.

Let me encourage you to make sure that Jesus Christ is **your redeemer**. God has revealed himself to you primarily through his Son, Jesus Christ, whose blood was shed to atone for **your sins**. Accept Him and His redemption today!

My Answers

Question 1

Various

Question 2

Heavens = heavenly bodies = sun, moon, stars. Essentially, everything that is in "the skies."

Interesting side bar: David did not view the sun, moon, and stars the way you do. Every human being before Galileo (c. 1600) viewed the sky from a geocentric viewpoint. Essentially, people thought that the stars were on some sort of canopy (or tent covering if you will), and that the sun and moon were flat disks going across (or in front of) that tent covering. Verses 4-6 reflect that type of understanding. After Galileo, we now understand and view the sun, moon, stars, and planets from a heliocentric viewpoint.

Question 3

- Line 1 = declare
- Line 2 = proclaims
- Line 3 = speech
- Line 4 = reveals—oooh, there's our word!
- Line 5 = speech
- Line 6 = voice heard

Question 4

The heavens are telling us that God is there and that He is glorious and all powerful.

Question 5

The telescope and the microscope

Question 6

Seeing heavenly bodies all the way to the edge of the universe with modern telescopes certainly expands our view of God's power and glory. But seeing things down at the cellular level with modern microscopes is where we really begin to gawk at unfathomable complexities that speak to us of a powerful intelligent designer—GOD!

Question 7

David was referring to the Mosaic law—the law given to Moses on Mt. Sinai.

Question 8

The Mosaic law is found in the books of Exodus, Leviticus, Numbers, and Deuteronomy. Note that the book of Genesis, while written by Moses, is not a part of the Mosaic law. Moses himself does not appear in the Scriptures until the book of Exodus.

Question 9

Most Bible scholars maintain that of the Mosaic law, only the Ten Commandments were written in stone. The Ten Commandments is the core part of the Mosaic law, which in a bigger sense is the Mosaic covenant between God and the Israelites.

Question 10

The law is perfect, sure, right, and pure.

Question 11

The law revives our souls, makes us wise, brings us joy, and enlightens our eyes.

Question 12

- Creation = candle light
- Mosaic law = flashlight
- Jesus Christ = stage spotlight
- Face to Face = bright sunlight

Question 13

Redeemer

Question 14

Very rarely do you see the word "redeemer" in the Old Testament. (Job 19:25 is the other very important OT "redeemer" verse.)

4

Psalm 98

Joy to The World

Psalm 98

[1]Oh sing to the Lord a new song,
    for he has done marvelous things!
His right hand and his holy arm
    have worked salvation for him.
[2]The Lord has made known his salvation;
    he has revealed his righteousness in the sight of the nations.
[3]He has remembered his steadfast love and faithfulness
    to the house of Israel.
All the ends of the earth have seen
    the salvation of our God.
[4]Make a joyful noise to the Lord, all the earth;
    break forth into joyous song and sing praises!
[5]Sing praises to the Lord with the lyre,
    with the lyre and the sound of melody!
[6]With trumpets and the sound of the horn
    make a joyful noise before the King, the Lord!
[7]Let the sea roar, and all that fills it;
    the world and those who dwell in it!
[8]Let the rivers clap their hands;
    let the hills sing for joy together before the Lord,
[9]For he comes
    to judge the earth.
He will judge the world with righteousness,
    and the peoples with equity.

The Study

Joy to the world! The Lord is come,
Let earth receive her King.
Let every heart prepare Him room,
And heaven and nature sing.
And heaven and nature sing.
And heaven, and heaven and nature sing.

Joy to the earth! The Savior reigns,
Let men their songs employ.
While fields and floods, rocks, hills, and plains,
Repeat the sounding joy.
Repeat the sounding joy.
Repeat, repeat the sounding joy.

He rules the world with truth and grace,
And makes the nations prove.
The glories of His righteousness,
And wonders of His love.
And wonders of His love.
And wonders, wonders of His love.

                                          Isaac Watts

Psalms of David Imitated

Isaac Watts (1674-1748) wrote over 600 English hymns in the early 1700s earning him the title "The Father of English Hymnody." From his birth, Isaac operated at a much higher level than you and I. He was learning Latin by age 4, Greek by age 9, and Hebrew by age 13!

Isaac's song writing career began at age 19 when his father challenged him to quit complaining about the dismal hymns being sung at church and write a decent one himself. The very first hymn that poured forth from Isaac's pen was from Revelation 5 and was titled, "Behold the Glories of the

Lamb." His congregation loved the hymn so much that they demanded that Isaac write a new hymn for church every week.

The hymns quickly piled up and eventually were published in two volumes—*Hymns and Spiritual Songs* (1709) and *Divine and Moral Songs* (1715). Around two dozen of these hymns are still sung today, some 300 years later! You'd likely recognize some of them. Perhaps the best known is "When I Survey the Wondrous Cross."

At this point, Isaac embarked on probably the largest hymn writing project of all time. He set out to write 150 hymns drawn from the 150 Psalms. The result was the volume—*Psalms of David Imitated* (1719). Here are the three most popular hymns from that volume:

- Psalm 72 – "Jesus Shall Reign Where're the Sun"
- Psalm 90 – "Our God, Our Help in Ages Past"
- Psalm 98 – "Joy to the World! The Lord is Come"

No doubt that last one caught your attention!

Yes, **the most recorded** Christmas carol of all time, "Joy to the World!" is taken directly from Psalm 98! It is uncanny how the thoughts and even the exact words of Psalm 98 were woven by Isaac Watts into one of our most beloved Christmas carols ever. When you get down to brass tacks, "Joy to the World!" is essentially **poeticized Scripture.**

Hopefully, our quick tour through Psalm 98 today will not only bless you but will cause you to sing "Joy to the World!" with a new love and appreciation every Christmas!

The Joy of Israel

Go ahead and get this Psalm organized by putting brackets around the four sections (1-3, 4-6, 7-8, 9) and labeling them "The Joy of Israel," "The Joy of All People," "The Joy of All Nature," and "The Lord Comes!"

Read Psalm 98:1-3.

Technically, the word "joy" does not appear in these first three verses.

1.   What line however insinuates a joyous attitude?

Quite a few of the Psalms put forth a list of the Lord's blessings to **national Israel.**

2. What line makes it crystal clear that the topic here is indeed what the Lord has done for **national Israel?**

3. What five things had the Lord done for national Israel according to these three verses? (Five verbs on the left, five direct objects on the right.)

_____	_____ _____
_____	_____
____ ____	_____
_____	_____
_____	_____ ____

The key to Psalm 98 is the pivot point in v. 3b. The Psalmist makes a turn and says that "all the ends of the earth" have seen the salvation which God had shown national Israel. Hence, Israel's joy can become the world's joy. Joy to the world!

The Joy of All Peoples

Read Psalm 98:4-6.

Now the word "joy" is popping up everywhere. Go ahead and circle every time a permutation of the word "joy" is used.

4. What three instruments are used to accompany people praising the Lord?

Of course, the main "instrument" in this passage is the human voice, which is far and away the most glorious instrument God ever created. Nothing is more sublime than the human voice with its boundless capabilities for expression and beauty. And God made **your specific voice** to redound praise back unto Himself.

Psalm 148 is very similar to Psalm 98. Call it a sister Psalm.

5. Name all the types of people mentioned in Psalm 148:11-13 that ought to praise the Lord.

I guess that covers just about everybody!

The Joy of All Nature

Now it is time for all of nature to pile on and "sing" joyfully.

Read Psalm 98:7-8.

6. What six parts of nature are said to join in praising the Lord?

The Christmas carol "Joy to the World!" does indeed follow Psalm 98 sequentially according to this outline:

- Stanza 1 = The Joy of all Peoples
- Stanza 2 = The Joy of all Nature
- Stanza 4 = The Lord Comes

What about stanza 3? Isaac Watts created it from Genesis 3:17-18. The key words and concepts in stanza 3 were "curse," "sorrows" (KJV), and "thorns." Remember, Watts never just made up words willy-nilly. His methodology was always **poeticized Scripture.**

But back in stanza 2, Isaac wrote: "while fields and **floods**, rocks, hills, and plains."

7. Why did Watts use the word **"floods"** instead of the word **"rivers"** found in v. 8 of most Bible translations?

Let's consult Psalm 148 again for a fuller list of "all nature singing."

8. Name the many parts of nature in Psalm 148:3, 7-10 that are called upon to praise the Lord.

That seems to cover just about all of nature!

Ultimately, **all peoples** and **all nature** are to praise the Lord because, according to one commentator, that is what they were made for. And even Jesus Himself on Palm Sunday said that if the people were restrained from praising Him, then the rocks themselves would cry out "Hosanna!"

The Lord Comes!

Read Psalm 98:9.

Bible commentators are in 100% agreement that this verse is a Messianic prophecy regarding Christ coming to judge the world—**an event that is still in the future!**

Christ's **first coming** was to save the world. Christ's **second coming** will be to judge the world. Jesus Himself claimed to be the executor of the Father's future judgment at the end of the age in John 5:22, 27-30.

This leads us to the next rather odd question.

9. Is "Joy to the World!" really a Christmas carol?

Wow. It seems like one of our most cherished Christmas carols isn't about Christmas at all. In fact, "Joy to the World!" has none of the nativity elements associated with all other Christmas carols. You know, things like the manger, Mary, Joseph, the angels, the shepherds, the star, the cattle (which are lowing), the inn-keeper, the wise men, and don't forget the baby Jesus (no crying he makes).

10. Is it okay to sing "Joy to the World!" at Christmas?

Of course! We can and will enjoy it immensely every Christmas. But this little extra understanding of where the song comes from and what it means will likely make it all the more special to you. But you might as well beat the Christmas rush and join with all heaven and nature in singing "Joy to the world, the Lord is come"—today!

My Answers

Question 1

"Sing to the Lord a new song" certainly implies a joyful spirit before the Lord.

Question 2

"To the house of Israel"

Question 3

- Done .... marvelous things
- Worked .... salvation
- Made known .... salvation
- Revealed .... righteousness
- Remembered........................ steadfast love

Question 4

Lyre, trumpets, horn

Question 5

Kings, all peoples, princes, rulers, young men, young women, old men, children

Question 6

Seas and sea creatures; land and land creatures; rivers; hills

Question 7

Isaac Watts was using the main translation of his era—the King James Version. The KJV says "let the floods clap their hands." All subsequent translations improved that line to "let the rivers clap their hands."

Question 8

Sun, moon, stars; sea creatures; fire and hail; snow and mist; stormy wind; mountains and hills; fruit trees and cedar trees; beasts and livestock; creeping things and flying birds

Question 9

Not really; it deals with Christ's second coming, not his first

Question 10

Of course it's okay! We can do anything we want!

5

Psalm 103
Healing

Psalm 103

[1]Bless the Lord, O my soul,
    and all that is within me,
    bless his holy name!
[2] Bless the Lord, O my soul,
    and forget not all his benefits,
[3] who forgives all your iniquity,
    who heals all your diseases,
[4] who redeems your life from the pit,
    who crowns you with steadfast love and mercy,
[5] who satisfies you with good
    so that your youth is renewed like the eagle's.

[11] For as high as the heavens are above the earth,
    so great is his steadfast love toward those who fear him;
[12] as far as the east is from the west,
    so far does he remove our transgressions from us.

The Study

We Sing That!

If I just threw out the words "Bless the Lord, O my soul," many Christians would say, "I know that phrase is in the Psalms . . . somewhere." Some might even correctly peg it as Psalm 103:1. And more than a few Christians would also blurt out, "Hey! We sing that at church!"

They would likely be referring to one of the most popular Christian songs of the past ten years, "10,000 Reasons" by Matt Redman. Here's the familiar opening chorus:

> *Bless the Lord, O my soul,*
> *O my soul,*
> *Worship his holy name.*
>
> *Bless the Lord, O my soul,*
> *O my soul,*
> *I worship your holy name.*

You could probably sing it a cappella right now!

Of course, older folks may also recall the Andre Crouch version from 1973. Andre's opening chorus quoted Psalm 103:1 exactly:

> *Bless the Lord, O my soul*
> *And all that is within me*
> *Bless his holy name.*

So in all likelihood, you are very familiar with the first verse of Psalm 103 and already have it bouncing around in your head.

I personally consider Psalm 103 to be **the most glorious Psalm ever**. The tone and loftiness of this magnificent Psalm is unrivaled in my opinion. And it is as theologically rich as it is beautiful.

We will focus our attention today on just a couple of important topics. But I encourage you to read and enjoy and be blessed by the glorious poetry of all of Psalm 103. And it ends the way it begins: "Bless the Lord, O my soul!"

Your Benefits Package

Read Psalm 103:1-5.

1. Why do you think preachers and commentators gravitate towards calling these verses "Your Benefits Package?"

2. Go ahead and fill in these easy blanks from vv. 2-5. Use only **one verb** and **one noun** in each line. Plus, let's simplify and use the word "sins" instead of "iniquity."

- _____ all your _____
- _____ all your _____
- _____ your _____
- _____ you with _____
- _____ you with _____

Wow! Read through that list again. That's a really impressive benefits package!

3. Would you say these benefits are primarily spiritual or primarily physical or kind of both?

So we have a fabulous benefits package from the Lord that seems to be primarily spiritual in nature. Nevertheless, it has one benefit that appears to be physical—"heals all your diseases." Let's delve deeper into that one. Healing can be a contentious and controversial subject in Christendom. But let's not close our eyes to it. Let's go ahead and tackle it today using

Psalm 103:3 as our jumping off point. It might be easier to resolve than you think.

The Healing Controversy

Christians can err two ways when it comes to the issue of "God healing today." Both errors stem from using some extreme words. Fill in the following with two extreme words that are dangerous to use in any context.

- God _____ heals
- God _____ heals

I'm sure you got it. One extreme is that God **always** heals today. There are good well-meaning Christians who believe this. Let's call them "hyper-healers." The other extreme is that God **never** heals today. Some well-meaning Christians believe this. Let's call them "non-healers."

4. How do each of these positions put God in a box?

5. Why is putting God in a box a bad idea?

As you can already surmise, probably a much better view is that God **sometimes** heals today.

But since "hyper-healers" use Psalm 103:3 as one scriptural plank in support of their view that God **always** heals, maybe we'd better take a closer look.

Hyper-Healers

Typically, a "hyper-healer" would begin with a little misdirection. He would focus your attention on the word "all." He might say something like this: "According to Psalm 103:3, buddy, God heals **all** your diseases. What don't you understand about the word **all**? **All** means **all**!"

Additionally, the hyper-healer would **not** alert you to the spiritual overtones of the whole benefits package.

The key probative question is this: Is Psalm 103:3 focusing on the healing of **literal physical diseases** or is it speaking **metaphorically** about healing or removing our sins?

I believe it is dealing **primarily metaphorically** about forgiving and eliminating sin. Elsewhere, in Psalm 30:2, Psalm 6:2, and Jeremiah 30:17, the Scriptures use the word heal **metaphorically** in the exact same vein.

But I think we really need to take a peek at two other critical verses that the hyper-healer would point to in support of his view that God **always** heals.

The first is the famous Messianic passage in Isaiah 53. The hyper-healer would draw your attention to the well-known phrase in v.5 "by his stripes we are healed." But you can see that the overall context deals with sin removal, not physical healing. The two immediate prior phrases in that verse, "He was wounded for our **transgressions**" and "He was crushed for our **iniquities**," are talking about the Savior taking on our sins. Indeed, in all of Isaiah 53, I count eight times that the Lord God is said to be laying the sins of the world on the future Messiah—Jesus. We really see no broad context of physical healing anywhere in Isaiah 53.

When the apostle Peter—in 1 Peter 2:24—quotes Isaiah's "by his stripes we are healed," Peter specifically contextualizes it as Jesus bearing our sins on the cross.

People can certainly legitimately disagree with me on this. But I would posit that all three passages—Psalm 103:3, Isaiah 53:5, and 1 Peter 2:24—are using the word "heal" in a **metaphorical** sense, applying primarily to sin removal, and **not physical healing.**

6. Do you think these healing passages should be interpreted metaphorically or literally or somehow both?

Non-Healers

At the other end of the spectrum, we have the "non-healers." They believe that God **never** heals today. The main issue with this view is that it runs counter to folks today who claim that God has indeed worked a miracle healing in their own life or in somebody they know.

Of course, reports of modern healings are many times hard to believe and harder to verify. Some healings appear iffy. Some seem explainable. Some seem downright goofy.

But, if you wanted to apply some extremely tough standards in verifying a true miracle healing today, you might require that the healing be:

- Recorded live
- Medically attested

The story of Duane Miller is one such miracle healing, which I've recounted in the next chapter. God suddenly and miraculously healed Duane while he was teaching Psalm 103, specifically verse 4. This miracle was **recorded live** in the Catacombs class at First Baptist Church Houston and **was medically attested** by the Houston medical community. Read it later when time permits. But for now, let me state categorically and unequivocally that **God sometimes heals today.**

Sin Removal Analogies

Let's finish by looking at one important final verse.

Read Psalm 103:12.

"As far as the east is from the west" is an analogy regarding God's removal of our sins.

7. But what exactly is an analogy?

8. How far is the east from the west?

9. What does this analogy imply?

There are only three sin removal analogies that I can find in the Scriptures. They are:

1. Whiter than snow—Isaiah 1:18
2. East to west—Psalm 103:12
3. Scapegoat—Leviticus 16:10

Remember, they are only analogies. They are pictures that help us understand that when God removes sin, **it is GONE!**

Let's try to determine which one we relate to the best.

10. Are there any Christians songs about "scapegoat?"

11. Are there any Christian songs about "east to west?"

12. Are there any Christian songs about "whiter than snow?"

Based on the song evidence, it seems like we gravitate to the "whiter than snow" analogy most of all.

Of course, the reality is that Christ's shed blood is what removes our sin from us as far as the east is from the west and what makes us whiter than snow. Jesus explicitly said in the upper room: "This is the blood of the covenant, which is poured out for many for the forgiveness of sins" (Matt. 26:28).

Accept Him and His free gift of pardon and forgiveness! And know that when God removes your sin, **it is GONE!** And know for certain that God sometimes still heals today!

My Answers

Question 1

- It has the word "benefits" in v. 2
- It does seem to be a list of benefits
- Modern Americans tend to think in terms of their employer's benefits package

Question 2

- **Forgives** all your **sins**
- **Heals** all your **diseases**
- **Redeems** your **life**
- **Crowns** you with **love**
- **Satisfies** you with **good**

Question 3

They are primarily spiritual. Of course, "heals all your diseases" definitely sounds quite physical. We are going to dig a lot deeper on that one. But the overall tenor of these benefits seems to be spiritual.

Question 4

- The first position—God never heals—seems to **limit** what God can do
- The second position—God always heals—seems to **dictate** what God must do

In either case, you end up saying that God must behave in a certain way, the way you've chosen for Him to behave.

Question 5

If you say that God only does "x," and then God does "y," who is going to look bad? A better policy might be to say that God can do anything he pleases rather than make hard and fast rules for God.

Question 6

You make the call

Question 7

An analogy is something that tries to describe or explain something else. It is not the real thing. It is an example that helps us understand the real thing.

Question 8

Sounds pretty far, some might call it infinity.

Question 9

When God removes your sin, **it is GONE!**

Question 10

No "scapegoat" songs

Question 11

No "east to west" songs

Question 12

There are plenty of "whiter than snow" songs—at least in the old hymnals. Here's some single lines from four golden oldies:

- *Are your garments spotless, are they white as snow?*
- *Would you be whiter, much whiter than snow?*
- *Now wash me and I shall be whiter than snow.*
- *Whiter than snow you may be today.*